ACHIEVE YOUR GOAL SOONER

COMPLETE WORKBOOK ON STRATEGIES TO OVERCOME PROCRASTINATION

BONUS: 7 NLP TECHNIQUES TO REWIRE YOUR BRAIN TO OVERCOME PROCASTINATION

MANJUSHREE MITRA

Contents

Dear Readers,

I hope this message finds you well. Reflecting on my life, I realize I have been a procrastinator for as long as I can remember. I've put off important tasks, delayed pursuing my dreams, and hesitated to express my feelings to those I care about. Now, at this juncture, I regret all the missed opportunities and unfulfilled potential.

I could have achieved much more, seen many places, and cherished precious moments with loved ones. But dwelling on these regrets won't change the past. Instead, I choose to focus on the present and the future.

That's why I decided to write this book. I want to share my journey of self-discovery and growth in the hope that others who struggle with procrastination will find solace and inspiration. I want to shed light on the reasons behind our tendency to delay and offer practical advice on breaking free from its grip.

It's always possible to make a change. There's still so much we can accomplish, so many experiences waiting to be embraced, and so much love to be shared. Let's not let procrastination hold us back any longer.

Procrastination can feel heavy, holding us back from reaching our full potential. It's easy to fall into the trap of delaying essential tasks, only to regret it later when we realize how much we could have achieved if we had just taken action sooner.

But here's the thing: we're all in this together. Procrastination is indeed something many of us struggle with at times. Whether it's delaying work for tomorrow or getting caught up in overthinking instead of taking action, we've all been there. And you're right; it can feel like we're held back by invisible chains, unaware of how much we can achieve if we break free from procrastination's grip.

But here's the thing: there is always time to change. We can use those feelings of regret and guilt as fuel to break free from procrastination and start taking action toward our goals. It's about recognizing that we have the power to shape our destinies, and every small effort we make today can lead to a brighter tomorrow. This book is about empowering others to overcome their struggles with procrastination and live a life of success and fulfillment.

Each page is filled with insights and strategies. Take charge of your life and unlock your true potential with powerful insights, proven strategies, and unwavering encouragement to break free from the debilitating grip of procrastination. Success and fulfillment are within reach for everyone, and by sharing our experiences. And by supporting each other, we can all achieve our goals and dreams. So, here's to a future filled with growth, achievement, and happiness for all who embark on this journey with us. Together, we can make it happen.

With regards,

Manjushree Mitra

Section 1

CHAPTER ONE

INTRODUCTION

You must have lived some part of your life while reading this book. Let me ask you some questions:

"Have you lived your life the way you wanted?"

Did you do what you had dreamt of?

Did you say what you wanted to convey to the person you loved?

If your answer is "Yes," Hurray!! You have lived your life to the fullest till now.

If you answer "No," ask yourself "WHY NOT." This caption is put in Capitals, not by mistake but on purpose. It is a huge question. There may be many answers, like

1. I needed more time.

2. I never thought I could do it.

3. What would society say?

4. What if I fail?

5. It's just a crazy thought.

There may be many more answers. But the concern is that your life is Incomplete. So many of the dreams are unfulfilled. At this moment, you would become defensive, blaming people and situations. But please understand this: whatever the case be, you did not do it.

A small back story.......

I had always procrastinated on work, mainly because I feared the outcome. I was good at writing poems and always wrote them at leisure. One day, in the college I studied, the college organized a poem-writing competition with a cash prize of 5000 rupees. My friends had always knew I had written some good poems and encouraged me to submit them.

When I was writing for myself in a diary, I was confident, but submitting it to college fest was an arduous task.

Encouraged by my friends, I took out my diary to select one poem to be submitted. But suddenly, all my poems are far from being good. Suddenly, all that I had written was just a scrap, and I was ashamed of having written them.

I tried to rewrite them, and with every rewriting, it seemed I was not even worthy of writing. I was sinking into depression. I used to cry behind the doors for being unable to write even a single line.

This was not imagination. I was not able to write anything. Writing what I used to write effortlessly, and emotions flew like water, was such a difficult job. Now I was afraid to write anything.

I was just wasting my time, and the deadline to submit the assignment was knocking on the door. I was trying to avoid college, as my friends would ask me if I had submitted my work. Suddenly, my friends became my enemies. I would not take their calls or go to college. Suddenly, 2-to 3 friends came to my house one day. As I opened the door, I was surprised to see them in front of me. I gave them a sheepish smile, trying my best to avoid their eye contact. For me, they were like the wolves waiting to devour me. I was waiting for them to hurl insults toward me and mock me.But contrary to that, they understood the pain I was going through. They had come determined to help me out of this dilemma. They did not ask me anything or advise me. They had just uttered a powerful line.

"It's just a journey, not a destination. "It was enough to see the sunlight through the dark room's skylight. Suddenly, I felt much happier and relaxed.

The next day was the last day of submission; I got up early, went to college, and submitted one of the old poems I had written. I did not receive the 5000 rupees prize money but was appreciated for what I wrote.

Key Takeaways from this Story:

1. Our internal fears, such as fear of failure and fear of judgment, often lead us to procrastinate and delay our work.

2. Setting excessively high standards can become a barrier to achieving our goals, as meeting these standards becomes increasingly challenging.

3. Peer pressure from well-meaning friends can inadvertently contribute to procrastination as we struggle to meet their expectations.

4. Success is not just about reaching a destination but also about the journey itself. Feeling overwhelmed by circumstances is counterproductive.

5. Participation and gaining experience are valuable in their own right, regardless of whether we achieve immediate success. Through participation, we accumulate the knowledge and skills that ultimately lead to success.

In this book, we will address these issues comprehensively:

1. The book's first part is about the mindset behind procrastination, exploring why people delay or avoid tasks altogether.

2. The book's second part will explore strategies to overcome procrastination and effectively manage our time.

Bonus:

Finally, in the 3rd part, 10 NLP techniques and tips for efficiently overcoming procrastination would be a bonus.

CHAPTER TWO

UNDERSTANDING PROCRASTINATION

Why do we delay our work when we really want to do it?

There may be many factors behind this. The mind is the most powerful thing in the world. It moves faster than the fastest known thing to man, that is, the speed of light.

Firstly, a thought form is created that we need to do this. There can be many examples.

You see a dog in terrible condition on the road; it just met with an accident and died. Now, the dog lover in you would want to prevent such accidents from occurring anymore. So, you decide that you will want to open a shelter for dogs. This thought is very nice and noble. You feel good about it. Now, you go home, and suddenly, other ideas come in for a reality check. Questions like How do I arrange the money? Will I get the required help? Will it affect my daily work and responsibilities? These questions pop into our little heads.

Suddenly, we feel overwhelmed by these thoughts. The sound and noble idea of opening a shelter becomes a faraway dream. Yes, it becomes a dream. The overwhelming thoughts have pushed the concept so far that it has become a dream.

Maybe this example is a bit away from reality; let's consider something we do daily. You wake up in the morning and plan to complete reading a book you downloaded on Kindle last night. This book has garnered accolades for its unparalleled excellence. But as you start reading the book, everything seems to be perfect. You read around fifteen pages, appreciating yourself for the choice you had made in the book. But suddenly, you felt it getting difficult to complete the pages. You were tempted to take up the phone and check social media accounts' messages, notifications, likes, and comments. Such great is the call of passion; you deviate from the path of work which you were determined to do. So, the book remains incomplete. You will feel frustrated and angry about yourself for not completing the book. However, you promise not to repeat this; again, but you repeat.

Let us take another example: you are a singer well-praised in your social network for the intricate voice and excellence that touches the soul of music. People around you always want you to use a better platform to showcase your talent. But you could never apply for the same as somewhere inside you, the heart trembles with trepidation, for it foresees the specter of failure looming large, accompanied by the disturbing notion that derision may befall you at the hands of others.

Psychologists call it "procrastination" - the act of delaying tasks that require our attention. But what lies at the heart of procrastination? It's a question worth exploring, for understanding ourselves is the first step towards overcoming this pervasive tendency. But procrastination is delaying essential tasks, often due to a reluctance to confront them. It manifests in various forms, from active procrastination, where individuals consciously postpone work to focus on other endeavors temporarily, to passive procrastination, a more insidious pattern driven by distractions and lack of motivation.

Active procrastinators possess a strategic approach to task management, utilizing the pressure of impending deadlines to fuel productivity. They recognize the value of balancing work with personal and social commitments, harnessing the benefits of delayed gratification. This form of procrastination, though deliberate, can paradoxically enhance time management skills and creativity.

On the other hand, passive procrastination stems from a subconscious aversion to work, often exacerbated by the dopamine-driven allure of social media and instant gratification. The constant stream of notifications and distractions hijacks our attention, leading us to procrastinate.

Dopamine, a brain chemical tied to pleasure and rewards, positively influences desire, happiness, and motivation. It can lead to addictive habits by taking over our brain's reward system. It's like a friend pushing us to keep doing something because it feels good, even if it's not always good for us. So, when dopamine kicks in, we might want more of whatever makes us feel good, whether it's food, games, or social media. Understanding how dopamine works helps us manage our cravings and make healthier choices in the long run.

So, how do we combat procrastination and reclaim control over our productivity? It begins with self-awareness and introspection. By identifying our procrastination triggers and patterns, we can develop strategies to mitigate them. Whether setting clear goals, creating structured routines, or implementing digital detoxes to reduce distractions, there are myriad ways to cultivate discipline and focus.

In the next chapter, we will understand the reason for procrastination.

CHAPTER THREE

PROCRASTINATION DETECTIVE

This chapter aims to uncover the reasons behind our procrastination tendencies. Are we genuinely delaying our work, and if so, why? Let us peel back the layers of human behavior to uncover the reasons behind our tendency to procrastinate. Along the way, we'll explore the different types of procrastinators and endeavor to discover which category we belong to. Prepare to explore the intriguing world of procrastination and discover surprising insights!

Procrastination, we all fight with it often due to many reasons. These reasons, like puzzle pieces, fit into broader categories, helping us make sense of our tendency to put things off. Whether it's the irresistible allure of distractions or the suffocating fear of not measuring up, these factors urge us to delay. But by recognizing these common reasons and embracing our human imperfections, we can begin to untangle the knots of procrastination and step into a brighter, more action-packed tomorrow.

1. **Fear of failure:** The fear of not being able to fulfill the expectations of others, always living under the anxiety of being criticized and looked down upon
2. **Perfectionism:** Keeping high expectations of oneself and creating a masterpiece in every project. Starting and finishing the task is only possible if all the criteria are met.
3. **Lack of motivation:** It's when the work is irrelevant to self-liking or self-development. It's just another project that has to be completed, for which no credit would be given to anyone.

4. **Poor Time Management:** Inefficient planning, delaying the start, and overwhelming tasks can lead to further delay. This may cause acute stress and sometimes leave the work incomplete.

5. **Distractions:** Social media, TV, and notifications are constant reasons for distractions, and they lead to procrastination.

6. **Task complexity:** Avoiding a task that has complexity in the form of the use of new technology, number of steps, or lack of knowledge in a particular area may lead to procrastination

7. **Self-doubt:** lack of confidence leads to procrastination. Self-doubt leads to overthinking, which causes the delay.

8. **Decision paralysis:** Lack of decision-making skills can lead to procrastination. Not being able to make decisions on the work process may delay the work.

9. **Lack of clear goals:** When what to achieve is not transparent, it would mean beating about the bush. These cause unnecessary delays in the work.

10. **Impulsivity:** An Impulsive person cannot concentrate on their work for a long time, which leads to delay.

Other factors may be small and also cause procrastination

1. **Health issues:** Physical and mental health is essential to performing work properly.

2. **Sleep deprivation:** Insomnia is mainly a reason for which people delay their work. Without proper rest, decision-making capacity is impaired.

3. **External pressure:** Too much peer pressure for perfection may create perfection syndrome. As discussed earlier, perfectionism causes procrastination.

4. **Overwhelming situations:** Similar to peer pressure, tight deadlines or sudden emergencies may cause delays.

5. **Delay/absence of Rewards:** If the rewards system is inappropriate, like in office politics, the deserving candidates are not given the credit and reward, and they will not be interested in the following projects. A lack of motivation can lead to procrastination.

6. **Lack of accountability:** When we don't feel compelled to confront consequences, we often fail to prioritize tasks, leading to procrastination.

7. **Disorganization:** A cluttered workspace leads to a lack of motivation to work. Required resources should be arranged in an organized manner for a better workflow. Otherwise, it leads to frustration and, ultimately, procrastination

8. **Perceived lack of resources:** A person who thinks they need more resources like material, skill, and time. For example, a person who is an office worker wants to write a book. But he delays it, thinking he does not have time. Many of us have dreams of becoming musicians, painters, or writers. Still, we procrastinate on this as we perceive a lack of resources, skills, and time.

9. **Unrealistic goals:** Completing an arduous task in a tight timeframe is impossible. Procrastination happens when there is a lot of work and time is very short.

10. **Negative self-talk:** Negative beliefs, lack of confidence, and self-doubt are primary reasons for procrastination. Not believing in one's abilities is the first step to procrastination.

Here is a questionnaire to help you understand if you are a procrastinator.

1. How often do you find yourself delaying or avoiding tasks that you must complete

   a. Rarely or never,
   b. Occasionally
   c. Frequently
   d. Almost always

2. When facing a challenging task, you tend to

   a. Tackle it head-on and get it done
   b. Delay starting, but eventually complete it
   c. Postpone it repeatedly, leading to stress
   d. Avoid it altogether and pass it to someone else

3. How do you prioritize tasks?

    a. Effectively prioritize and manage time well
    b. Prioritize but struggle to follow through consistently
    c. Often, you find yourself overwhelmed and uncertain about where to begin
    d. Tend to ignore prioritization completely

4. Do you wait until the last minute to start a critical task

    a. Rarely or Never
    b. Occasionally
    c. Frequently
    d. Almost always

5. How do you feel about deadlines

    a. They motivate me to start and complete tasks
    b. I sometimes need the pressures of a deadline to focus
    c. Deadline stress me out
    d. I miss the deadline; I go into hiding.

6. Are you a perfectionist when it comes to work

    a. I strive for excellence and still appreciate my own work
    b. I have perfectionist syndrome, but I can be flexible
    c. I am not satisfied with my work. I redo it many times
    d. I struggle to start my work as I believe I do not have enough understanding to make this work perfect.

7. How do you handle long-term projects

    a. Break them into smaller, manageable tasks and plan accordingly
    b. Start with good intentions, but not consistent
    c. Often feel overwhelmed and delay starting and completing the project
    d. Avoid long-term projects.

8. Do you seek support/assistance when needed?

    a. Yes, I actively seek help when necessary
    b. I sometimes hesitate but eventually ask for help
    c. I prefer to work alone and may avoid seeking help
    d. I rarely ask for help, even when struggling with the task

9. How do you typically react When you have a deadline approaching?

    a. Plan and start early to ensure sufficient time for completion.
    b. Start working closer to the deadline but manage to finish on time.
    c. Do it at the last minute
    d. Avoid the deadline altogether.

10. Do you set goals?

    a. I regularly set goals and achieve them
    b. I set goals but struggle to follow them consistently

    c. Setting goals is overwhelming.
    d. I rarely set goals

12. Do you find yourself distracted when trying to focus on tasks?

    a. Rarely or never, I can maintain focus easily.
    b. Occasionally, but I regain my focus quickly
    c. I am distracted till the last moment
    d. Almost always, I miss my deadline because of it.

13. How do you handle tasks when you find an uninteresting portion of the project

    a. I do the boring and uninteresting thing first
    b. I mix up the exciting and boring portions of the project
    c. I do the interesting portion first, then take a long time to finish the uninteresting portion.
    d. I avoid the uninteresting portion and try to push it on others

14. Are you aware of the reasons for delaying your project

    a. I know why I am postponing them
    b. Yes, but sometimes I fail to address the root cause
    c. Yes, I get distracted; it happens unconsciously
    d. No, I am not aware

15. How do you feel after your work is delayed due to your distractions

    a. I am frustrated, but I use it as motivation
    b. I am disappointed but I promise not to let it happen again
    c. Stressed and anxious, hoping for things to improve
    d. Anxious but looking for an escape path through excuses.

16. How would you describe your overall attitude towards work?

    a. Positive and motivated
    b. Generally positive, but with occasional challenges
    c. Mixed, sometimes motivated, other times distracted.
    d. Can never concentrate

Outcome:

1. Suppose you have a maximum A as an answer. Congratulations. In that case, you are a successful, highly motivated, and enterprising person.
2. If you have a maximum B as an answer, you don't have a significant problem of procrastination. You are successful but need motivation from time to time.
3. If you answer with a maximum C, you are a procrastinator. You need to consciously use the methods described further in the book.
4. If you have a maximum D as an answer, you are a critical procrastinator, where clinical help is advised.

This book is a journey from C to A, where you can be enterprising and successful. People with maximum D need to consult a professional counselor for one-to-one sessions. They can also benefit from this book, but going to a counselor is highly recommended.

The questionnaire in this chapter helps identify and explore procrastination habits.

The next chapter will explore the mentality of delaying work and how to avoid it.

In the upcoming section, we'll understand the reasons behind procrastination and explore effective methods to overcome it. By understanding the roots of your procrastination tendencies and implementing practical strategies, we aim to pave the way for achieving optimal outcomes. Together, we'll embark on a journey of self-discovery and growth, forging a path toward greater productivity and fulfillment. Join us as we unravel the mysteries of procrastination and unlock the secrets to unlocking our full potential.

SECTION 2

UNDERSTANDING REASONS BEHIND PROCRASTINATION

"Do not wait; the time will never be 'just right.' Start where you stand, and work with whatever tools you may have at your command, and better tools will be found as you go along." - Napoleon Hill

CHAPTER FOUR

EMBRACING RESILIENCE

In this chapter, we're diving into how the fear of failure can make us put things off. But guess what? There's a secret weapon against it: Resilience. The thought of failing can sometimes make us freeze up, feeling unsure and hopeless from the start. It's like a heavy cloud hanging over us, making us doubt ourselves and lose confidence. But we shouldn't let that fear hold us back. Instead, we can see failure as a chance to learn and grow. By facing our fears head-on, we can break free from that dark cloud and build our confidence, knowing that every setback is another step toward success. So, don't let fear stop you—embrace it as part of the journey to reach your goals.

Yet, in such fear, there is an opportunity to embrace resilience. Resilience is the hidden strength that enables us to be back from setbacks, to persevere in the face of adversity, and to rise above our doubts and insecurities.

Rather than allowing fear to dictate us, we can reframe our mindset. Failure doesn't define us; it's the first step toward learning, growing, and eventually succeeding. So why be afraid of it? Every setback becomes a valuable lesson, every challenge an opportunity for personal development.

Embracing resilience means acknowledging our fears but refusing to let them control us. It means recognizing that failure is not a destination but a temporary detour on the road to success. By cultivating resilience, we empower ourselves to face our fears head-on, take risks, and pursue our goals with unwavering determination.

Our greatest glory is not in never falling,
but in rising every time we fall." – Confucius

Here is a questionnaire given for every question. Please rate yourself from 1-5,

1- Strongly disagree

2- Disagree

3- Neutral

4- Agree

5- Strongly Agree

1. I avoid taking on challenges
2. The thought of failure stresses me out
3. I fail to accept failures and face them.
4. I get anxious by the feeling that people will laugh at me if I fail.
5. I set unrealistically high standards to avoid the possibility of failure.
6. I usually downplay my achievements to avoid meeting expectations.
7. I need to redo the work many times for my satisfaction.
8. I delay my work, thinking I cannot concentrate enough on the work.
9. I take failures to my heart and go into my cocoon.
10. After failure, it becomes difficult to start any new project.

Scoring:

• Add up the rating and find out how much you score

• If you score high, that means you have a high fear of failure

• If your score is:

10-20: Low fear of failure

20-30: Moderate fear of failure

30-40: High fear of failure

40-50: Very high fear of failure

Methods to Overcome Fear and Embrace Resilience:

1. **Stop Negative thoughts:** We all have that little voice inside our heads that loves to whisper doubts and fears, telling us we'll fail. It's like society planted it their way back in our childhood. It's time to quiet that annoying voice and replace it with one that cheers us on. Because deep down, we know we're capable of more than we give ourselves credit for. So, we must silence the negativity and start believing in our potential. I have explained NLP methods in the book's third section. It will help to remove the negative thoughts and unblock our potential.

2. **Break down your task:** Break your task into bite-sized pieces. Focus on completing one small part at a time before moving on to the next. Each accomplishment boosts confidence and propels you forward. Breaking it down will make the workload more manageable and less overwhelming. It's a simple yet effective strategy to maintain momentum and ensure steady progress. So, take it one step at a time, and soon, you'll be amazed at how quickly you reach the finish line.

3. **Love the process, not the outcome:** Enjoy the journey, not just the destination. When you divide your project into manageable tasks, focusing on realistic and achievable goals, you'll find that the satisfaction comes from the process, not just the end result. As the saying goes, "Live one day at a time, for life is made up of these small moments." So, embrace each step along the way, relishing your progress with each small accomplishment. It's in the journey that true fulfillment is found.

4. **Build resilience:** Develop a comforting sentence or a ritual to comfort yourself in case of failure. You might also adopt a reassuring phrase like, "This setback is not the end of my journey; I will bounce back stronger."

These positive affirmations serve as anchors during challenging times, helping you cultivate resilience and navigate through adversity. Practice incorporating these affirmations into your daily routine to strengthen your resilience muscle and thrive in the face of setbacks. These positive affirmations are vital to build resilience. Build resilience by creating a comforting ritual or mantra to soothe yourself during failure. Whether going for a walk, hitting the gym, or taking a vacation, find what brings you solace and rejuvenation.

5. **Visualize Success:** Picture your success by creating a vision board. Envision yourself standing tall and accomplished, not just in a year but also in five and even ten years. It's all right if you're unsure how to reach those goals right now. Trust that with good intentions, success will find its way to you. It's like setting sail on a voyage without knowing the exact route—the journey will unfold as you go. So, dream big, visualize your success, and let your intentions guide you toward a future filled with achievements and fulfillment.

6. **Celebrate each Milestone:** Celebrate every step forward in your journey, no matter how small. Just like every drop contributes to the vastness of the sea, each success in your project improves the overall quality. Take, for instance, a YouTuber who starts with just a few followers. When they reach 100, 1,000, and eventually 1 million followers, each milestone deserves celebration. These celebrations mark achievements and fuel motivation for the next goal. So, remember to celebrate, whether it's a tiny victory or a major triumph. These moments pave the way for even greater success.

7. **Develop a strong sense of purpose:** Having a clear goal is like having a guiding light in the darkness. Take successful companies as example—they all have a vision and a mission that drive them forward. This vision gives them a strong sense of purpose. Let's say a YouTuber has a vision of reaching 1 million viewers to spread awareness about a social cause. Even if they face setbacks or delays along the way, their purpose keeps them motivated.

Let's take another example. Imagine a teacher who is passionate about empowering students to succeed. Their purpose is to positively impact each student's life, helping them reach their full potential. Even if they encounter challenges in the classroom, like difficult lessons or disruptive behavior, their sense of purpose drives them forward. They know that every effort they make contributes to the greater goal of shaping young minds and the future. With this strong sense of purpose, they remain resilient and dedicated to their mission, no matter their obstacles. Nothing can deter you from reaching your goals when your purpose is more significant than the obstacles.

8. **Being part of a community of like-minded people:** Being part of a community of people who share your interests and experiences can be incredibly valuable, especially when you face challenges or setbacks. Instead of dealing with problems alone, reaching out to others who understand can make a big difference. Don't isolate yourself—venture out and seek ideas and support, no matter how small. Your community can offer insights to help you understand the root of the issue and find solutions together. So, don't hesitate to lean on your community when you need it—they're there to help you navigate challenging times and become more assertive on the other side.

9. **Grow from Setback and Adapt to Change:** When you experience failure, you can turn it into an opportunity for growth by adapting to change. This allows you to turn roadblocks into stepping stones towards success. When we encounter setbacks, we have a choice: to let them defeat us or to use them as opportunities for growth. Thomas Edison famously said, "I have not failed. I've just found 10,000 ways that won't work," referring to his numerous attempts at inventing the light bulb. Each "failure" taught him valuable lessons that eventually led to his success.

Setbacks can provide valuable insights into practical strategies for personal growth. Through our experiences, we gain the strength and wisdom to conquer any challenge that comes our way. For instance, if a business venture doesn't succeed as planned, instead of giving up, we can analyze what went wrong, adjust our strategy, and try again. This willingness to learn and adapt helps us bounce back stronger and paves the way for more outstanding achievements in the future.

10. **Practice Mindfulness:** Meditation and spiritual practices like mantra repetition can boost resilience by nurturing faith in a higher power. One can find solace and strength to endure life's challenges by connecting with the divine. For example, during moments of stress or uncertainty, prayers or meditation can provide a sense of calm and reassurance. Spiritual connection inspires and guides, instilling belief in a greater purpose beyond difficulties. Moreover, surrendering to a higher power cultivates acceptance and trust in the journey, allowing one to navigate adversity with grace and resilience. Integrating spiritual practices into daily life can ultimately contribute to inner peace, grit, and an unwavering sense of stability in the face of life's trials and tribulations.

CHAPTER FIVE

BE IMPERFECT!!!! PERFECTION IS A MYTH

"Perfectionism is a thief of time. It robs you of productivity by insisting that everything must be flawless before you can move forward." - Brian Tracy.

Perfectionism in many people is associated with the tendency to be number one. Better than others and best in whatever you do. To an extent, it is good as it drives you to improve every moment, but, on the other hand, it can be very toxic. Toxic to the power of infinity where you will not be able to start or finish the work.

You're unique, with your talents and quirks that make you, well, you! But ever since we were little, there's been this pressure to measure up to others. Whether it's from our parents, teachers, or even relatives, we constantly feel like we must be better than everyone else.

This constant comparison game can mess with our heads. Instead of just doing our thing and chasing our dreams, we get stuck in this cycle of trying to be perfect. We keep tweaking and redoing our work, thinking it'll never be good enough.

But guess what? It's time to break free from that cycle. You are who you are, and that's awesome! Your work is unique because it's yours—it reflects your thoughts, talents, and experiences. So, embrace your individuality and trust that you can make a difference uniquely.

How would you know that you have perfection syndrome:

Here is a questionnaire given for every question; please rate yourself from 1-5,

1. Strongly disagree

2- Disagree

3- Neutral

4- Agree

5- Strongly agree

1. I set unrealistic goals and get frustrated when I cannot achieve it

2. For me, another person's opinion and criticism matter the most.

3. I do not delegate my tasks; I have to do it all by myself

4. I repeatedly redo the same work until I am satisfied.

5. I am not satisfied with other people's work

6. I sacrifice other activities to make that one project done with perfection

7. I feel anxious if the work doesn't go as planned and there is uncertainty.

8. Most of the time I try to find fault with my work

9. I struggle to start or finish my work due to high set standards.

10. I compare myself to others and feel inferior to them.

   • Add up the rating and find out how much you score

• If you score high, that means you have high perfection syndrome

10-20: Low perfection syndrome

20-30: Moderate perfection syndrome

30-40: High perfection syndrome

40-50: Very high perfection syndrome

High perfection syndrome is toxic and can lead to anxiety and frustration

How do we avoid perfectionism:

1. **High standard vs Perfectionism:** We must approach our tasks with dedication and integrity but also understand that striving for perfection isn't necessary. Excellence comes from sticking to our values and continuously improving rather than chasing an unattainable ideal.

   Our imperfections are what make us human and unique. Take the Mona Lisa painting, for example. Despite its missing eyebrows, it's considered a masterpiece. This shows us that greatness isn't about being flawless; it's about embracing our imperfections and finding beauty in them. So, let's focus on doing our best while accepting that we're not perfect. It's this acceptance and appreciation of our flaws that genuinely makes our efforts extraordinary.

2. **Stop Focusing on Failure:** Living in the failure of the past is killing oneself multiple times. So, stop dwelling on the fear of failure. Instead, channel your energy towards fostering a mindset focused on growth and progress. Embrace a positive outlook and view setbacks as opportunities to learn and improve. Doing so allows you to tap into your full potential and pursue your goals with confidence and determination. Perfectionists often magnify their mistakes and imperfections. So, accepting anything less than flawless results is complicated. This tendency to obsess over perceived flaws leads them to redo tasks repeatedly, draining valuable time and energy. I've personally experienced the frustration of this

perfectionist mindset, which has often resulted in the loss of productive hours, days, and even months. At times, it's led me to feel so disheartened that I've considered abandoning projects altogether.

3. **Reframe negative thinking:** Breaking free from negative self-perception and constant self-criticism is crucial for unblocking our true potential. Many of us, overly critical of ourselves, often use perfectionism as a shield, justifying our relentless pursuit of flawlessness. Despite saying, "I am a Perfectionist," deep down, we struggle with feelings of inadequacy and a never-ending quest for self-improvement. The thought of "I am not good enough" constantly haunts us, driving the need for constant validation and the urge to redo tasks until they're perfect. But by embracing self-acceptance and understanding that imperfection is part of being human, we can be free from self-doubt and embark on a journey toward genuine growth and fulfillment.

4. **Don't be a Control freak:** Perfectionism often emerges from a deep-seated desire to have everything under control, including how others perceive us and the situations we encounter. This need for control stems from a fear of uncertainty and a longing for acceptance and approval. It's like constantly striving for an unreachable standard because, deep down, we doubt our worth. Sometimes, this doubt is rooted in our upbringing, like having strict parents or teachers who instill in us a sense of never being good enough. This constant pressure to measure up can leave us feeling like we must be flawless in every aspect of our lives.

5. **You are unique!! Stop Comparing:** "You are one of a kind, with your own set of strengths and quirks that make you uniquely you. Yet, from a young age, the pressure to measure up to others, whether from parents, teachers, or relatives, has seeped into our consciousness. The constant comparison game, where we feel we must outdo everyone else, can slowly erode our sense of self.

Instead of simply pursuing our goals, we find ourselves trapped in a cycle of perfectionism, endlessly tweaking and redoing our work in a futile quest for flawlessness. This consumes our time and distances us from our dreams, leaving us overwhelmed and disconnected. But it's time to reclaim your narrative. Remind yourself, 'I am who I am, and that's enough.' Your work carries your unique imprint, reflecting your perspective, talents, and experiences in a way only you can. Embrace the beauty of your individuality, and trust in your ability to make a meaningful impact.

• 29 •

CHAPTER SIX

TURN ON THE AIRPLANE MODE

**"The greatest enemy of progress is
not stagnation but distraction." - Tony Robbins.**

Starting work can be challenging when distractions like phone calls or messages interrupt your concentration. Afterward, you may feel guilty about wasting time, which can further affect your focus. It's important to remember that this is a common occurrence, and there are ways to make it easier. Simplifying tasks into manageable steps can help you approach them more effectively and feel more productive. Simplifying tasks into manageable steps can help you complete them more effectively and feel more productive by breaking down your work into smaller, achievable goals.

Here are some more questions to ask yourself:

1. Are you among those who want to check the social media the first thing in the morning?
2. Do you spend more time than you intended on your phone before going to bed, scrolling through social media feeds, or watching videos?
3. Do you have to check every notification that pops up on your screen, even if it's not urgent?

4. Do you experience anxiety or a sense of unease when you are separated from your phone, even for a short period?

It's not uncommon to feel this way, as smartphones and social media have become ubiquitous in our daily lives. However, it's essential to recognize the negative impact that this behavior can have on our mental health, including increased stress and anxiety, decreased productivity, and disrupted sleep patterns.

But acknowledging these feelings is just the first step towards improvement. It's essential to take concrete actions to reduce phone usage, such as setting limits on screen time, turning off notifications, or taking breaks from social media. Reading, meditating, or hanging out with family and friends can also help you handle stress and anxiety.

By taking these steps, you can create a good relationship with your phone and social media, allowing you to be more present and focused on the things that matter most in your life.

Daily, we encounter various distractions that can steal our attention and time. Some of these distractions are harmless, such as attending social events, spending time with our beloved pets, or chatting with family members. However, these activities may take up some of our productive time. But, some of these distractions can improve our concentration power. Social interactions trigger oxytocin release, dubbed the "happy hormone," which promotes relaxation, focus, and attention, thus boosting productivity. However, excessive time spent on our phones might negatively impact our dopamine levels. One hormone that functions as a neurotransmitter is dopamine. This hormone is essential to the reward system in our brains. Our brains release dopamine when we do enjoyable tasks, like using our phones, making us feel good.

However, spending too much time on our phones can cause an imbalance in our dopamine levels, which can lead to addiction, anxiety, and other negative consequences.

Let's understand the effect of Dopamine on us.

Dopamine is a neurotransmitter that is secreted in the brain and acts as a chemical transmitter. It's necessary for,

1. It acts as a reward system. It is released when a positive activity is undertaken, like finishing work, watching a movie, or finishing a novel. It's important to reinforce positive behavior through the reward system.

2. Dopamine also helps in the movement of the body. Inadequate dopamine leads to Parkinson's disease.

3. Dopamine regulates mood and emotions. Irregularity in Dopamine is the leading cause of mental diseases like schizophrenia or mood-related disorders.

4. Dopamine acts as a motivator for goal-oriented work

5. Dopamine helps in concentration of work, cutting down on distractions

6. Dopamine also determines the time; attention can be sustained.

In today's digital age, our lives are flooded with constant information, thanks to the proliferation of mobile devices, tablets, social media, and television. These devices have a common feature - notifications for likes, comments, and shares. These notifications act as a powerful motivator, stimulating the release of Dopamine in our brains, which gives us a sense of accomplishment and pride. This rush of Dopamine can be a positive thing to a certain extent because it helps to build confidence and self-worth. However, we should also be aware of the potential adverse effects of becoming too reliant on these notifications for validation.

But if these mediums are overused, it causes over-secretion of Dopamine, which causes an imbalance of the neurotransmitter. It also causes attention deficit. You continuously focus on the trigger, like the notification sound, for the release of Dopamine. It's also causing FOMO(Fear of Missing Out).

What was once a tool of pleasure turns into addiction.

Dopamine oversupply can cause a loss of cognitive power in the mind; you cannot concentrate on anything, and the urge to go back to what gives you happiness (social media) is very high. This is one of the main reasons for the delay in work. This leads to procrastination.

Some methods to avoid this:

1. **Unfollow and Mute Notifications:** Stop your phone or laptop from ringing. To minimize interruptions and maintain focus, it's imperative to take proactive measures such as unfollowing those not-so-necessary distractions and muting notifications on your devices. Prioritize your workload. Allocating specific times throughout the day to check messages and make phone calls. Reserve these periods for essential communications while avoiding non-urgent interruptions during work hours. Establishing boundaries and managing distractions effectively can optimize productivity and dedicate uninterrupted time to your tasks.

2. **Prioritize your phone calls:** Not every phone call is urgent. While friendships are valuable, it's essential to recognize that not every call requires immediate attention. By setting a polite voicemail message requesting callers to leave a voice note explaining their reason for calling, we can prioritize important matters while acknowledging the significance of connections. Those closest to us will understand our need for focus. At the same time, others may wait for a callback, ensuring our time is spent efficiently and meaningfully.

3. **Use Application timer:** Just go to the settings on your phone and set realistic time limits for the phone application. As humans, we all need breaks to rejuvenate, but it's important to place restrictions on excessive screen time. By setting these limits, we can balance productivity with self-care and promote healthier habits in our digital interactions. We can use time sets for each application we know that consumes maximum time. It's important to adhere to the rules and not just change them at our convenience.

4. **Have a designated workplace:** The presence of higher officials in the office environment cultivates a sense of enterprise and drive among employees. This office structure's accountability and sense of responsibility naturally diminish the urge to check social media,

resulting in a more focused work atmosphere. However, outside of the office setting, such constraints are often absent. Therefore, it is crucial to designate a dedicated workspace away from distractions. Augmenting this space with inspirational messages displayed prominently on walls or tabletops and incorporating motivational wallpapers on computers and laptops can enhance productivity and maintain focus. Staying focused on goals by fostering a positive, ambitious environment helps to stop distractions.

5. **Use focus technique:** It is impossible to focus for an extended time. It's essential to break the total work time into short periods for enhanced productivity; the Pomodoro technique can be employed for this purpose. Focus for 25 min on stress and then take a 5-minute break. After 4-5 sessions of this type, a more extended break of 45 minutes to 1 hour can be taken. Please don't use the phone or check your messages during the 5-minute interval. You can do it for a more extended break. The 5-minute break is for some stretching, eye movement, and drinking water, which would help better focus in the next session.

6. **Accountability partner:** Collaborating within a team offers numerous advantages over solitary work. Having an accountability partner significantly reduces distractions, fostering a more focused work environment. With multiple individuals involved, motivation emerges organically, transforming tasks into enjoyable activities. Consequently, the prevalence of distractions diminishes substantially when compared to working alone.

7. **Reward Yourself:** To increase productivity and motivation, it's essential to understand how to activate the brain's reward system. Imagine you start writing a book. Each time you finish a chapter, you earn some points. It's not just about getting closer to your big goal; it's also a chance to earn points. These points aren't just numbers; they're your tickets to small indulgences, like guilt-free screen time. Let's say you finish a chapter—that's worth 10 points. And what are those 10 points? They mean you get 10 minutes of screen time without guilt. This approach makes it easier to tackle that next chapter because you're not just inching toward your goal; you're earning rewards along the way. This system taps into something powerful: the joy of making progress and the excitement

of getting rewarded. It's not just about checking things off your to-do list; it's about feeling fulfilled and satisfied as you hit those milestones. And when productivity and rewards go hand in hand like this, it creates a cycle of motivation that keeps you moving forward with energy and excitement.

8. **Journal your day:** As the day comes to a close, it's helpful to take a moment to reflect on how it unfolded. Start from the moment you wake up, recounting each step you took until bedtime. This simple practice gives you a bird's-eye view of your day. By jotting down these details, you gain valuable insights into how you spend your time. You can thus identify patterns of procrastination and productivity and areas where you could improve. It becomes easier to spot activities that didn't contribute much to your day, helping you make better choices in the future. This habit also boosts self-awareness, empowering you to take control of your time and make the most out of each day. Commencing with the awakening hour, delineating each step from freshening up to nourishing meals, this practice serves as a reflective exercise, offering a panoramic view of the day's progression. By meticulously recording these details, one not only gains insight into their daily performance but also unveils productivity patterns and areas of potential improvement. Identifying unproductive activities becomes easy through this comprehensive log, enabling one to make informed decisions to optimize time utilization.

CHAPTER SEVEN

POWER OF SMALL STEPS

Have you ever had one of those days where your to-do list feels more like a mountain than a checklist? Trust me, we've all been there. It's like you're staring at this pile of tasks and don't know where to begin. But what if I told you there's a secret weapon to conquer that mountain? It's all about breaking it down into bite-sized pieces. Would you eat a whole watermelon in one bite? No, right? You'd take it one juicy slice at a time. Well, your tasks are like that watermelon. They might seem vast and daunting initially, but once you start slicing them up, they become much more manageable.

So, instead of getting overwhelmed by the sheer size of your to-do list, start breaking it into smaller chunks. It's like turning that intimidating mountain into a series of manageable hills. Suddenly, what seemed impossible becomes doable.

So, the next time you feel buried under a mountain of tasks, remember this simple trick: Break it down. Take a step back, grab your metaphorical knife, and start slicing. Before you know it, that towering mountain will be a distant memory, and you'll be standing tall on the summit of productivity.

Let me discuss some necessary steps to break a towering work into small, manageable pieces. We would take the example of planning a road trip to understand the journey from being overwhelmed to wearing the crown of success.

1. **Analyse your work:** Whether writing a report, studying for an exam, or decluttering your space, you must have a roadmap. It's about knowing your destination before you even start the journey. For example, imagine

you're going for a road trip to a beautiful destination. Before hitting the road, you would plan your route, where you're going, how you'll get there, and what stops you'll make. Well, tackling tasks is just like planning a road trip.

Think of your project as a road journey with numerous stops on the way. Plotting your course on a map to achieve success is a must. Each task is like a stop along the way, and knowing where you're headed helps to navigate with purpose and direction. So, before you hit the road of productivity, please take out a moment to map out your route. Knowing where you're going and watching as each step brings you closer to your destination. You're the driver of your own journey, so buckle up and enjoy the ride!

2. **Set your goal:** Do you often find yourself feeling unmotivated and directionless in life? It's time to set clear goals and have a destination in mind. Having a goal in sight can be incredibly motivating and give you a sense of direction. Instead of wandering aimlessly, you'll know precisely how to reach your destination. Furthermore, setting goals will help you stay focused on what's important and hold yourself accountable. By promising to reach your destination by a specific time, you'll feel a greater sense of responsibility and be more likely to take action. Don't let procrastination hold you back any longer - set your sights on a clear destination and start working towards it today!

Dividing your goals into smaller tasks is like dividing your journey into smaller steps. It makes the whole thing seem less overwhelming and more straightforward to tackle. Plus, seeing progress along the way motivates you to keep going.

3. **Prioritize your work:** Deciding which tasks to do first is like making a to-do list for a big project. Start by checking for any urgent deadlines, like finishing a report by the end of the week. Then, focus on the tasks that will help you reach your primary goals, like gathering research or making a plan.

Think about which tasks depend on each other, too. For example, you can only write the report once you've gathered all the necessary information. So, prioritize those tasks accordingly to avoid getting stuck.

It's also helpful to tackle the critical and easy tasks first. Maybe that means organizing your notes or sending out meeting invites. Getting these done early can give you a sense of accomplishment and keep you motivated.

But don't overload yourself with too many high-priority tasks at once. It's crucial to balance your workload so you don't feel overwhelmed.

If you're working with a team, ensure everyone knows the priorities. This way, everyone can pitch in and work together towards the same goals.

By prioritizing tasks like this, you can stay organized, progress, and succeed in your project without feeling stressed.

4. **Allocate time and Resources:** Imagine you're getting ready to cook a big meal. Like in the kitchen, allocating time and resources for sub-jobs in your project is like having all your ingredients and tools lined up before you start. It's super handy because you know exactly what you need and how long each part will take. This way, you won't have to pause halfway through because you're missing something, and you'll have a clear idea of when you can move on to the next step. It's like having a well-organized recipe for success! So, by planning and allocating time and resources wisely, you're setting yourself up for smooth sailing and getting things done without any unnecessary delays.

5. **Remember to have your Victory dance:** Completing each task in your project is like hitting a target in a game – it's a moment to celebrate! Whether finishing a report, meeting a deadline, or solving a challenging problem, each accomplishment is worth cheering for. Imagine yourself reaching the finish line of a race, feeling the excitement of getting each mini-goal. By acknowledging these victories, you're boosting your spirits and motivating yourself to keep going. So, take a moment to pat yourself on the back, give yourself a round of applause, and revel in the joy of progress – because every small step brings you closer to your ultimate goal!

6. **Power of Single-tasking:** Once you've organized your tasks, focus on one thing at a time and forget about the big picture for a moment. Why? Thinking about the whole project simultaneously can make it seem overwhelming, like a vast mountain to climb. That feeling of being overwhelmed can lead to anxiety and fear, which can drain your motivation in no time. Instead of letting fear take over, concentrate on one task at a time. It's like focusing on one puzzle piece at a time instead of trying to see the whole picture all at once – you're giving all your energy and attention to what's right in front of you. This way, you're reducing pressure on yourself and increasing your chances of completing tasks on time.Trust the plan you've made and the tasks you've assigned. There's no need to doubt yourself or redo the planning. Believe in your abilities and the roadmap you've created – it's your path to success. So, take a deep breath, focus on your goals, and confidently tackle each task.

7. **Navigate the journey with flexibility:** Life often throws unexpected situations, like surprises or changes we didn't see coming. But being flexible means we're adaptable, like a skilled surfer riding the waves. Instead of resisting these surprises, we adjust our approach and go with the flow.

So, when unexpected challenges happen, there's no need to panic! Instead, we can see them as opportunities to pivot and find new ways to tackle them. Whether it's a sudden change in plans or someone on our team getting sick, staying flexible helps us develop creative solutions.

Think of it as dancing – sometimes, we have to improvise our steps to keep up with the music. By being flexible, we can overcome obstacles and stay on track toward our goals. So, let's keep an open mind, stay quick on our feet, and remember that every twist and turn is just another part of our journey to success.

CHAPTER EIGHT

TACKLING ONE TASK AT A TIME

Let's take it this way: you're a juggler in a circus, and your job is to keep multiple balls in the air simultaneously. Each ball represents a task or activity you need to accomplish. At first glance, juggling so many balls at once might seem impressive, but let's take a closer look.

When juggling, your attention is divided among all the balls flying through the air. You must constantly shift your focus from one ball to another, ensuring no drop. Similarly, when we multitask in our daily lives, we divide our attention among different tasks, switching back and forth between them.

Now, here's where it gets interesting. "Our brains cannot multitask effectively. Instead of focusing on multiple tasks simultaneously, our brains perform better when concentrating on one task at a time." Instead, they rapidly switch attention from one task to another. It's like trying to juggle too many balls – one will fall sooner or later.

When we multitask, we might feel like we're being productive, but in reality, we often end up overburdened by taking on too many tasks at once. Our performance on each task tends to suffer because we must give our full, undivided attention to one study. It's like trying to write an email while talking on the phone and watching TV – chances are, the email will be full of typing errors, and again, you won't remember what the person on the phone said.

Not only does multitasking decrease the quality of our work, but it can also increase stress levels and make us feel overwhelmed. It's like trying to juggle too many balls at once – eventually, something will come crashing down, and it's usually our mental well-being.

Instead of multitasking, experts recommend focusing on one task at a time, giving it your full attention until it's completed or until you reach a natural stopping point. This approach, known as single-tasking, allows you to fully immerse yourself in the task at hand, leading to better concentration, higher quality work, and reduced stress.

So, while multitasking might seem like a superpower, it's more of a myth. Like the juggler in the circus, we're better off focusing on one ball at a time if we want to achieve true mastery and avoid dropping the ball.

You know that feeling when you're scrolling through social media, and you see everyone else seemingly living their best lives, traveling to exotic places, attending exciting events,

and you start to feel like you're missing out? That's FOMO – the fear of missing out – creeping in. It's like there's a party happening, and you're worried you're not invited.

And then there's anxiety, that little voice in your head constantly whispering about all the things you need to do, all the deadlines looming over you, and how you should probably be doing them all at once to keep up. It's like having a hundred tabs open in your brain, each demanding your attention.

So, what do we do? We start multitasking, trying to keep up with everything and everyone, afraid that if we focus on just one thing, we'll miss out on something else. It's like juggling too many balls simultaneously, hoping none will drop.

But here's the thing – multitasking might seem like the solution to our FOMO and anxiety, but it's making things worse. When we try to do too much at once, our attention gets divided, and we end up not giving any one thing the focus it deserves. It's like trying to watch three movies simultaneously – you might catch bits and pieces of each, but you won't fully enjoy any of them.

That's why focusing on one thing at a time is so important. It's like giving each task its spotlight on stage – that way, it gets the attention and effort it needs to shine.

So, the next time FOMO creeps in, or anxiety knocks at your door, take a deep breath, remind yourself that it's okay to focus on one thing at a time and permit yourself to fully immerse yourself in whatever you're doing. Trust me, you'll feel more present, more productive, and much less frazzled.

1. **Task Prioritization:** Are you overwhelmed with the number of tasks that need to be completed? One simple solution is to create a to-do list! Take a moment to jot down all the tasks. Instead of letting them consume you, organize them in order of urgency and importance. Start with the most pressing and work your way down the list. By focusing on one task at a time, you'll be able to give each one the attention it deserves. Don't let the chaos of unfinished work drive you crazy; take control of your day with a to-do list!

2. **Setting Boundaries:** Are you tired of constantly getting distracted and feeling unproductive? Imagine a cozy home with designated rooms for different activities, where you can cook in the kitchen, relax in the living room, and get work done in the study. What if I told you that setting specific time boundaries for different tasks and avoiding distractions during those times could significantly increase your productivity? Whether you need to answer emails or work on your latest project, give each task a slice of uninterrupted attention and watch your productivity soar.

3. **Time Management Tricks:** Have you ever felt like there aren't enough hours in the day? The Pomodoro Technique can help you with this problem. It's like having your personal time wizard. Break your work into bite-sized chunks. Work on one task briefly, then treat yourself to a well-deserved break. This way, you can keep your focus sharp and energy levels high without getting lost in the multitasking maze.

4. **Stop Distractions:** Silence your phone, close unnecessary tabs on your computer, and carve out a little oasis of calm where you can let your creativity flow uninterrupted.

5. **Mindfulness Magic:** Close your eyes and take a deep breath. Experience a weightless moment as you sink into the present. When there is urge to multitask, gently guide your focus back to the here and now. Remind yourself that taking things one step at a time is okay, like strolling through a sun-dappled forest instead of sprinting through a crowded city street. With some practice, you'll find that mindfulness is like a superpower - helping you stay grounded, focused, and ready to tackle whatever life comes your way.

CHAPTER NINE

SECRETS OF TIME MANAGEMENT

Do you ever find yourself putting off tasks, telling yourself you'll do them later, only to feel overwhelmed by the mounting to-do list? That's where time management comes in. It's like having the power to conquer procrastination!

Time management is about controlling and using your time wisely to get things done efficiently. Precious moments and hours are waiting to be discovered in a treasure trove. Take the time to explore and embrace them, as you never know what treasures you might find. With adequate time management, you can accomplish your goals and dreams.

But how do you do it? It's about setting priorities, breaking tasks into smaller, manageable chunks, and creating a plan of action. Think of it as crafting a roadmap for your day, guiding you through each task with purpose and clarity.

By managing your time effectively, you beat procrastination and unlock possibilities. You'll feel more in control, less stressed, and capable of dealing with life's challenges.

Effective time management is like conducting a symphony, not juggling tasks. Managing time can spell the difference between feeling overwhelmed and being in control in a world where every second counts.

Take the Pomodoro Technique, for instance —Effective time management involves carving out moments for both work and personal pursuits. But time management isn't just about work; it's about carving out moments for the things that truly matter, whether spending time with your near ones pursuing hobbies or simply taking a moment to enjoy life's little joys. So, let's embrace the power of time management to compose a life that's harmonious, balanced, and brimming with possibilities.

Here are some strategies to manage time for more productivity and reduce procrastination.

1. **Make a to-do list:** Plan your next day for a few minutes before going to sleep. Set yourself up for success every day, starting from waking up. First things first: let's talk about food. We all know how much time cooking can take, especially if you're trying to figure out what's for breakfast, lunch, and dinner on the fly. So, why not decide ahead of time? Plan your next day's meals, and ensure you have all the groceries you need. It'll save you a lot of time and stress. Next is time blocking, a fancy way of saying you will assign a specific time to different tasks throughout your day. For example, if you know you want to spend an hour doing yoga, block that time off in your schedule. The same goes for taking a shower, having lunch, and any other activities you have planned.
And here's the kicker: make sure you're setting aside dedicated "work time" each day. Work time is when you grow your skills, work on your dreams, or earn money. Break it down into smaller tasks, like tackling the most crucial job first, checking emails, and wrapping up with making your to-do list for the next day.
By taking a little time to plan, you're setting yourself up for a smoother, more productive day. So, before you hit the hay tonight, take a few minutes to map out your tomorrow. Your future self will thank you for it!

2. **Prioritize your job:** Consider your to-do list as a spectrum, ranging from the most critical tasks to the least important ones. At one end, you've got the big tasks crucial for your personal growth and advancement in life. It might include going to work, working on that career-boosting project, or investing time learning new skills to help you level up.

On the other end, you've got the time-wasters – the tasks that don't add value to your life and might even take you away from your goals.

Scrolling through Instagram or Facebook might feel good, but it's not moving you forward in the grand scheme. That's why keeping these activities in check and limiting them to just a tiny part of your day is essential.

And then there's the middle ground – the tasks that may not directly contribute to your personal growth but are essential for your overall well-being. This could be as simple as chatting with your best friend or taking a moment to relax and recharge. While these tasks may not directly impact your career or goals, they're essential for maintaining your social, emotional, and physical health.

By categorizing your tasks based on their importance, you can prioritize your time and energy on the things that truly matter while making room for the little indulgences that make life sweet. It's all about finding that balance and staying focused on what's truly important to you.

3. **Set Goals:** First things first: Before diving into any task, clearly understanding what you're aiming for is crucial. Think of it like setting your GPS coordinates before embarking on a journey. Without a destination in mind, you'll just be wandering.

That's where SMART goals come in. These are like your road signs, guiding you toward success:

- Specific: know what you want to achieve. The more detailed, the better.
- Measurable: Measure outcomes to track progress effectively, ensuring goal attainment clarity.
- Achievable: Keep it realistic – setting goals out of reach can lead to frustration.
- Relevant: Align goals with values and long-term objectives for a meaningful achievement journey.
- Time-bound: Set a deadline to keep yourself accountable and motivated.

Now, let's talk about the Japanese art of "Ikigai". It's all about finding your life's purpose and waking up each day with a new, renewed energy and drive. Setting goals taps into this same principle, making your work more meaningful and helping you avoid the trap of procrastination. How do we set goals? It's like building a staircase to your dreams:

- Start with your vision for life – what do you want to achieve?
- Define your mission – how do you plan to make it happen?
- Break it down into smaller goals – what do you want to accomplish in 10 years, one year, one month, and even one day?
- For example, say your vision is to donate 25 lakhs to those in need in the next ten years. To make it happen, you'll need to earn 2.5 crore in that time (donation equals 10% of the income). That breaks down to roughly 6600 per day. Suddenly, your goal becomes like a tiger chasing you – you can't afford to be lazy!

By setting clear, actionable goals, you turn your vision into a roadmap for success. So, start plotting your course toward a brighter future!

4. **Multitasking is a myth:** Multitasking, oh, the allure of it! It's like chasing after a mythical unicorn, believing it'll lead us to productivity nirvana. But let's be honest: how often does multitasking deliver on its promises?

   Picture this chaotic scene: you're trying to answer emails, whip up dinner, and converse with your partner simultaneously. It's like trying to juggle flaming torches while riding a unicycle on a tightrope. Impressive? Maybe. Effective? Not so much. The truth is, we're not wired to multitask. Our brains struggle to focus on multiple tasks simultaneously, leading to distractions, mistakes, and chaos. It's like dividing your attention into too many pieces, resulting in a mess of half-completed tasks.

   Instead, focusing on one task at a time allows us to give it our full attention and effort, leading to better results in less time. It's like putting all your energy into mastering one skill rather than spreading yourself thin across multiple endeavors. So, the next time you're tempted to multitask, remember: it's not about doing more; it's about doing better. Give yourself the gift of focus and watch your productivity soar.

5. **Difficult work first:** An old saying is, "Start with the hardest task first; that way, the rest of the day will be a cakewalk or at least a stroll in the park." This quote captures the essence of tackling complex tasks head-on. It highlights the potential for a more manageable day once the most demanding job is out. While the specific attribution may be elusive, the sentiment rings true for many striving to maximize productivity.

   So, face the job's most significant and complex part first, with complete determination and power. You are filled with new vigor and enthusiasm at the start of the work. These attributes would help you to sail through this difficult phase with ease. It's like taking down the dragon, which is spitting fire when you want to enter the cave filled with gold. With each stroke of determination, the dragon is brought to the ground before it devours you. The mighty dragon is procrastination, which consumes precious productivity.

   So once the most challenging part is done, with renewed self-confidence, the rest of the work is completed in the set time frame. So, one must do the most demanding work first thing in the morning when the energy level is the highest. As the day passes and the energy level goes down, we can move on to tackling less crucial tasks.

6. **Pomodoro technique:** One of the most beloved time management techniques is the Pomodoro method; let me tell you, it's a game-changer! This technique was Developed by Francesco Cirillo in the 1980s and got its name from the Italian word for tomato, "Pomodoro."

   Here's the lowdown: you break your work time into bite-sized chunks of 25 minutes, called Pomodoro's, followed by a short 5-minute break. It's like slicing up your workday into manageable pieces, making it easier to stay focused and productive.

   Research has shown that the average person's attention span lasts about 25 minutes, so dedicating this time to a single task ensures maximum concentration and efficiency. And those 5-minute breaks? They're like mini-vacations for your brain, allowing you to recharge and return refreshed and ready to tackle the next Pomodoro.

After completing four Pomodoro, treat yourself to a more extended break of 15-20 minutes. It's the perfect reward for your hard work and dedication. By breaking your tasks into Pomodoro, you're reducing procrastination and increasing your concentration and productivity. It's a simple yet powerful method that helps you get things done effectively and without distractions. So, grab your timer and try—you'll be amazed at what you can accomplish!

7. **Delegate your work:** Delegation of work is your secret weapon to unlock peak productivity and efficiency. Picture this: by entrusting tasks to capable team members, you're not just lightening your load but empowering others to shine in their areas of expertise. It's a win-win scenario that propels your team towards success. Imagine the satisfaction of seeing tasks completed seamlessly, deadlines met with ease, and goals surpassed—all thanks to the power of delegation. By harnessing the diverse talents within your team and effectively communicating expectations, you're laying the groundwork for a collaborative and high-performing work environment. So, why wait? Embrace delegation as your superpower, and watch your team soar to new heights of achievement and fulfillment.

REST: YOUR SECRET WEAPON

Let's discuss the importance of taking breaks in our busy work schedules. Your brain suddenly feels like mush when you grind away at your tasks. Yeah, that's your cue to step back and recharge.

Think of it like this: your brain needs downtime to dream, just like your phone needs a charge to keep running smoothly. It's all about finding that sweet spot between work and rest. Taking time off helps you beat procrastination.

The brain is in resetting mode when you take a break. You get a chance to rest up and come back to your tasks with a fresh perspective. It's like getting a mental recharge that helps break the cycle of boredom and procrastination.

Also, taking breaks helps prevent burnout. If you keep working without stopping, you can get tired and stressed. And that makes procrastination worse. Taking some time off allows you to recharge and stay motivated to get stuff done.

Speaking of motivation, sometimes all you need is a little break to get back in the groove. When you step away from your work for a bit, you can do things that inspire or make you happy. That boost of positivity can reignite your enthusiasm and make it easier to dive back into your tasks.

Plus, breaks are great for sparking creativity. Allowing your mind to wander during non-work moments can lead to a burst of creativity, enabling you to come up with fresh and innovative ideas. You might even find solutions to problems you've been struggling with, all because you took some time to relax and let your brain do its thing.

Taking breaks also helps you stay focused when you return to work. If you keep pushing yourself without downtime, your concentration can fade. But when you take a break, you return with renewed energy and attention, making it easier to stay on track.

Reflecting on your goals and priorities is a good idea during your time off. Setting yourself up for success starts with a little bit of self-reflection.

And let's not forget about stress. Procrastination significantly increases your stress levels, particularly with upcoming deadlines. But by taking breaks, you can manage your stress and prevent it from getting out of control. A little relaxation can go a long way in helping you stay calm and focused.

It's also essential to take care of your physical health. Procrastination can sometimes lead to neglecting things like exercise and eating right. But when you take time off, you can prioritize your well-being and indirectly boost your productivity and motivation.

Lastly, set some boundaries between work time and time off. Do not check your work emails or messages during your break; it will help you fully disconnect and recharge. By sticking to your boundaries and using your time off wisely, you'll reap the benefits of beating procrastination with ease.

Let us discuss strategies to effectively take time off from work to relax and increase productivity:

1. **Schedule Regular Breaks:** Take regular breaks into your work schedule, short breaks every hour, or longer breaks like not working throughout the day. You can do activities that would relax and rejuvenate you, whether taking a walk, practicing mindfulness, or simply stepping away from your work environment.

2. **Plan Vacations and Getaways:** Taking longer breaks, such as vacations or weekends away, disconnects you from work, allowing time to rejuvenate with enjoyable activities and quality time.

3. **Implement the Pomodoro Technique:** Employ the Pomodoro Technique: Work for 25 minutes, then take a 5-minute break for efficient time management. After completing four cycles, take a longer break (15-30 minutes). This structured approach can help maintain focus during work periods while ensuring regular relaxation breaks.

4. **Practice Mindful Relaxation:** Incorporate mindfulness into your relaxation time to promote mental and physical well-being. It can include meditation, deep breathing exercises, progressive muscle relaxation, or simply being present in the moment. Mindful relaxation techniques can reduce stress, improve focus, and enhance productivity when you return to work.

5. **Engage in Hobbies and Leisure Activities:** Dedicate some time to pursuing hobbies and leisure activities that bring you joy and fulfillment. It can be reading, painting, gardening, playing sports, or cooking. Investing in activities you love can provide a much-needed break from work-related stress and help recharge your creative energy.

By implementing these strategies, you can effectively take time off from work to relax and recharge, ultimately increasing productivity and overall well-being in the long run.

CHAPTER ELEVEN

MICRO-TUNING BEHAVIOUR FOR SUCCESS

"Micro-control" implies a granular level of attention to detail, suggesting that even minor behaviors and choices can significantly impact outcomes. It encourages individuals to pay close attention to their thoughts, emotions, and actions, recognizing that each tiny decision contributes to their success or failure.

Elaborating on this concept involves consciously monitoring and adjusting your behavior in various situations to align with your goals and values. It may include practicing self-discipline, maintaining a positive mindset, managing time effectively, and cultivating healthy habits.

Mastering self-management skills can enhance their productivity, resilience, and overall well-being. It's about taking ownership of your actions, making deliberate choices, and consistently striving for improvement. Ultimately, the small, incremental behavioral changes lead to significant long-term success.

1. **Early Risers:** Early mornings boost productivity and curb procrastination. Rising early in the morning builds discipline and focus, setting a proactive tone. The quiet ambiance fosters deep work, enhancing efficiency. Establishing a routine reduces decision fatigue, keeping you on track. With higher energy levels, tasks are approached with vigor, minimizing procrastination. Prioritizing self-care in the morning boosts mood and well-being. Planning time ensures a smooth, productive day ahead. Better sleep quality complements early rising, unlocking sustained productivity and success. So, as the old saying fits here: c try to implement it for better productivity and reduce procrastination

2. **Exercise/stretch daily:** Stretching is inversely proportional to stress. Exercise can alleviate stress and enhance productivity. Moving our bodies, whether through walking, jogging, or any form of physical activity, releases feel-good chemicals in our brains called endorphins. Endorphins help alleviate stress and improve our mood, making us more relaxed and focused. Additionally, regular exercise promotes better sleep, sharper concentration, and increased energy levels, all contributing to enhanced productivity throughout the day. So, get up and go for a Run!!

3. **Meditate:** Taking just 30 minutes to meditate can unlock profound insights into our capabilities. Through meditation, we can connect with our true selves by silencing our minds and focusing inward. It provides clarity, helping us understand our strengths, weaknesses, and untapped potential. By this, we gain a deeper understanding of our abilities and limitations, empowering us to make more informed decisions and pursue our goals with confidence. Meditation also cultivates a sense of calm and presence, enabling us to navigate challenges with greater resilience and clarity. Invest in yourself with just 30 minutes of meditation and unlock your full potential.

4. **Proper Nutrition:** Fueling our bodies with a balanced diet packed with fruits, veggies, whole grains, lean proteins, and healthy fats. It is necessary to unlock peak brain power and vitality. These nutrient-rich foods fuel optimal brain function, sustained energy levels, and well-being. By nourishing our bodies with these wholesome ingredients, we supercharge productivity and sharpen concentration, paving the way for success in both work and life.

5. **Adequate sleep:** Relaxation is essential for productivity. Relaxation is like hitting the reset button for our productivity. During REM (rapid eye movement) sleep, our minds and bodies truly unwind and recharge. Think of it as the body's maintenance mode - repairing tissues, processing emotions, and storing memories.

Without enough REM sleep, we're like a phone running on low battery, struggling to function at our best. By prioritizing relaxation and ensuring we get quality REM sleep, we're giving ourselves a power boost, ready to face whatever challenges come our way with renewed energy and clarity.

REM is needed to achieve complete relaxation of mind and body.

6. **Continuous learning:** Reading books is necessary.

Reading books fuels our minds, keeps us motivated, and keeps us growing. It's not just a hobby; it's a necessity for staying sharp and inspired. Power-up for our minds is essential for continuous growth and motivation. It's a journey that takes us to new worlds, teaches us valuable lessons, and keeps our spirits high. To keep up, aim to read at least 12 books a year - that's just one per month. Whether

a gripping novel or an inspiring self-help guide, each book fuels our curiosity, broadens our horizons, and equips us with fresh insights to navigate life's twists and turns. So, grab a book, dive in, and let the magic of reading propel you forward!

<u>A reader lives a thousand lives before he dies. The man who never reads lives only one."</u> - George R.R. Martin

7. **Effective communication:** Practicing active listening, clear articulation, and empathy in your interactions with others to build strong relationships, resolve conflicts, and foster collaboration. Listening carefully, speaking clearly, and understanding others' feelings help build good relationships and solve problems. When we listen carefully, we show respect and interest in what others say. Speaking clearly helps in making sure that everyone understands our message. Understanding how others feel, called empathy, helps us connect with them better and respond kindly. These skills are essential in both personal and work life. They help us work well with others, solve problems, and get along smoothly. So, we can build solid relationships and work together effectively by listening, speaking clearly, and understanding others.

8. **Self-Reflection:** Regularly reflect on your actions, achievements, and areas for improvement to identify strengths and weaknesses, set meaningful goals, and make necessary adjustments to progress toward success. Take time to think about what you've done and achieved and where you can improve. Look at what you're good at and what you need to work on. Then, set goals that matter to you and figure out what you need to do to reach them. Make changes along the way to keep moving

forward. It helps you grow and improve at what you do, making it easier to succeed. Reflecting on your actions and goals is like steering your ship - it keeps you on course toward your dreams.

9. **Work-Life Balance:** It's essential to maintain a balance between work, personal life, and leisure activities to prevent burnout, nurture relationships, and sustain long-term success and happiness. Find a balance between work, personal life, and fun activities to avoid feeling overwhelmed, keep relationships strong, and ensure lasting happiness and success. It's like juggling different parts of your life to keep them all in harmony. Taking time for yourself, spending time with loved ones, and pursuing hobbies are essential for your well-being. This balance prevents burnout, strengthens connections, and lays the foundation for a fulfilling life. Remember, it's not just about working hard—it's about living well and enjoying every aspect of your life journey.

10. **Positive Mindset:** Cultivate a positive attitude, optimism, and resilience in the face of setbacks or challenges. They should be considered opportunities for growth and learning rather than obstacles to success. Nurture a sunny outlook, hope, and inner strength when things get tough, seeing them as chances to grow and learn, not roadblocks. By staying positive, you bounce back stronger from setbacks, like a spring that stretches but doesn't break. Every challenge becomes a lesson, every stumble a step forward. With this mindset, you paint life's canvas with bright colors, turning hardships into stepping stones toward success. So, keep smiling, believing, and growing—because the best views come after the most challenging climbs.

SECTION 3

REWIRE YOUR BRAIN WITH

NEURO- LINGUISTIC PROGRAMMING

TO OVERCOME PROCRASTINATION

CHAPTER TWELVE

HOW DOES NLP HELP TO OVERCOME PROCRASTINATION

Let's understand this: You've got this big task like a giant school project or something from work. But instead of tackling it head-on, you keep saying, "I'll do it tomorrow." Sound familiar? Here's the deal: Your brain is like a tricky friend playing a game with you. It's about choosing between what feels good right now and what's a drag. When you think about doing that task, it feels like a chore – that's the "pain" part. But doing something fun, like scrolling your Instagram or chilling with friends, feels incredible – that's the "pleasure" part.

So, your brain is like, "Hey, why bother with the boring stuff when we can have fun right now?" And that's when procrastination kicks in. It's like your brain's way of protecting you from the hassle. But here's the twist: It's still today when tomorrow comes, right? So, you end up putting it off again... and again. That "tomorrow" never seems to show up! Your brain is tricking you into avoiding the hard stuff forever.

But here's the secret: If you want to beat procrastination, you've to live in the now. Instead of pushing things off, tackle them head-on today. Once you get started, it's like breaking free from a trap – and trust me, you'll feel fantastic for it!

So next time your brain whispers, "Eh, do it later," tell it, "No, I will do this now!"

NLP offers powerful tools to tackle procrastination by rewiring how we think and act. First, it helps identify the root causes of procrastination, whether fear of failure or overwhelming. Then, techniques like anchoring or reframing change our mindset, replacing procrastination triggers with motivation and clarity. Visualizations and goal-setting exercises create a clear path forward, breaking tasks into manageable steps. By addressing underlying beliefs and habits, NLP empowers us to overcome procrastination, replacing hesitation with action and doubt with confidence. It's like giving our minds a tune-up, enabling us to unlock our full potential and quickly achieve our goals.

1. **Anchoring** - Harness Your Inner Motivation: Anchoring is like having a secret weapon against procrastination. It can help you overcome the habit of delaying or putting off tasks. Picture a moment when you felt unstoppable and associate it with something simple, like squeezing your fist gently while repeating a motivating phrase. The next time procrastination strikes, trigger this anchor to summon that powerful feeling and dive into your tasks headfirst.
2. **Reframing** - Have you ever felt overwhelmed by your to-do list? Reframe those tasks as exciting opportunities for growth and achievement! Instead of dreading them, focus on the positive outcomes and personal development they'll bring. Suddenly, what seemed daunting becomes a chance to shine.
3. **Visualizations** - Close your eyes and envision yourself conquering your tasks effortlessly – that's the power of visualization! Picture every detail, from starting each job quickly to basking in the glow of accomplishment. By visualizing success, you'll boost your confidence and banish procrastination.
4. **Meta-Modelling** - Rewrite Your Inner Dialogue: Challenge those thoughts that whisper, "You can't do it" or "It's too hard." Replace them with empowering beliefs like "I am capable" and "I thrive under pressure." You'll conquer procrastination and unlock your full potential with a positive mindset.
5. **Anchoring Future Pacing** - Connect with Future Success: Transport yourself to the future and feel the satisfaction of completing your tasks. Anchor positive feelings to motivate action in the present moment. With your eyes on the prize, procrastination doesn't stand a chance.

6. **Swish Pattern** - Imagine yourself giving in to procrastination, then swiftly replace that image with a vivid vision of yourself taking action and making strides toward your goals. With a simple mental switch, you'll transform inertia into momentum and procrastination into productivity.

7. **Anchoring Motivation Strategies** - Identify the things that motivate you and connect them to your tasks. Whether it's the excitement of achieving something, the prospect of receiving recognition, or the pursuit of personal fulfillment, let those motivations drive you forward and eliminate any tendency to procrastinate.

Let us understand these in detail. In this section, we will go details into the strategies mentioned above and try to free ourselves from the chains of procrastination, which not only eats away at our productivity but also refrains us from leading the life we desire

CHAPTER THIRTEEN

HARNESS YOUR INNER MOTIVATION

Imagine you're sitting at your desk, feeling incredibly motivated and productive. You could have just finished a task you've been putting off for ages, and you're riding that wave of accomplishment. At that moment, you create an anchor—a mental link between this feeling of motivation and a specific physical gesture or word.

Let's say you clench your fist lightly as a physical gesture. As you do this, you repeat a positive affirmation like "I am focused and unstoppable." You repeat this gesture and affirmation a few times, soaking in the feeling of motivation and productivity.

Now, here's where the magic happens. The next time you find yourself procrastinating, staring at a daunting task, and feeling completely unmotivated, you can use this anchor to shift your mindset. Clench your fist again and repeat your affirmation, and instantly, you'll tap into that reservoir of motivation and productivity you anchored earlier.

It's like having a secret weapon against procrastination, a way to summon your most motivated self whenever you need it most. And the best part? You can create as many anchors as you like, tailored to different situations or feelings you want to amplify. So, whether you're facing a challenging project or struggling to get started on your to-do list, your anchors guide you back on track.

Let's break down anchoring in an office work context using an example:

Imagine working on a project at your desk and suddenly feeling a burst of motivation and productivity. You're fully engaged, focused, and making significant progress. In this moment, you can create a mental anchor to capture this state of motivation and productivity.

1. **Identify the Anchor:** Choose a specific physical gesture or word to serve as your anchor. For example, you might lightly tap your desk with your fingertips or say "focus" to yourself.
2. **Associate with the State:** As you experience the peak of motivation and productivity, perform your chosen anchor gesture or say the anchor word. Repeat it a few times while fully immersed in the productive state.
3. **Repeat and Reinforce:** Repeat this process whenever you feel motivated and productive. You reinforce the connection in your mind by consistently associating the anchor with this positive state.
4. **Triggering the Anchor:** You can activate your anchor when you procrastinate or find it challenging to focus on your work. Perform the physical gesture or say the anchor word to access the state of motivation and productivity you've anchored.

For example, let's say you're overwhelmed by a daunting task and tempted to procrastinate. You can gently tap your desk with your fingertips (the anchor gesture) or quietly say "focus" to yourself (the anchor word). By doing so, you activate the mental anchor you've created, instantly accessing the motivated and productive state associated with it.

With practice, anchoring becomes a powerful tool that helps you overcome procrastination and stay on track with your work. It is a quick and effective way to shift your mindset and reengage your focus whenever distractions or procrastination arise.

CHAPTER FOURTEEN

TRANSFORM YOUR TASK INTO TRIUMPHS

Do you ever find yourself drowning in a sea of tasks at work? It can feel like you barely keep your head above water. Is your to-do list overwhelming? "What if we could transform this situation into an opportunity for growth and achievement?"

Picture yourself at your desk, staring at a lengthy list of tasks to be completed by the end of the week. Instead of feeling stressed, take a deep breath and see each task as an opportunity to shine.

First things first, let's talk about reframing. It is like putting on a new pair of glasses that can open your eyes to a whole new world of possibilities. Instead of seeing your tasks as burdens, you see them as stepping stones to something bigger and better.

Take, for example, that big project your boss just handed you. Instead of thinking, "Oh no, this will take forever," let's reframe it as an opportunity to showcase your skills and expertise. Picture yourself delivering an impressive presentation or receiving praise from your colleagues for a job well done. Suddenly, that daunting project becomes a chance to shine and prove yourself in the workplace.

Now, let's talk about focusing on the positive outcomes. Instead of getting bogged down by the details of each task, think about the bigger picture. What will completing these tasks mean for you and your career? Will it help you develop new skills, build stronger relationships with your coworkers, or even lead to a promotion down the line?

Imagine being assigned to lead a team on a new project. Instead of feeling intimidated by the responsibility, focus on the positive outcomes. Think about how successfully leading this project could boost your leadership skills, improve your standing within the company, and open up new opportunities for advancement.

Finally, let's talk about personal development. Every task, no matter how small, has the potential to help you grow and learn. Instead of seeing them as chores, view them as opportunities to expand your knowledge, skills, and abilities.

Suppose you are assigned the responsibility of planning a corporate event. Instead of seeing it as a tedious chore, think about how it will challenge you to sharpen your organizational and communication skills. You might even discover a hidden talent for event planning that you never knew you had!

So, the next time you feel overwhelmed by your to-do list, remember this: Each task is a chance for growth, achievement, and personal development. By reframing them this way, you'll tackle them with renewed energy and enthusiasm. You might amaze yourself with all that you can achieve. Each task is a chance for growth, achievement, and personal development. By reframing them this way, you'll tackle them with renewed energy and enthusiasm. And who knows? You might surprise yourself with how much you can accomplish! On your team. Instead of focusing solely on the workload, think about the potential outcomes of the report. It's a chance to present valuable insights, influence decision-making, and contribute to the success of the project or initiative.

By reframing the task in this way, you're not just checking off boxes on your task list; you're stepping into the role of a strategic thinker, problem solver, and valued team member. So, the next time you encounter a daunting office task, remember to see it as an opportunity to shine and make a real difference in your workplace.

CHAPTER FIFTEEN

SET SUCCESS BEFORE IT HAPPENS:

Imagine you have a pile of paperwork sitting on your desk and feeling overwhelmed by the thought of tackling it. You can use visualization to help overcome procrastination and boost your motivation.

1. **Create a Mental Movie:** Close your eyes and imagine yourself sitting at your desk, calmly and confidently sorting through the paperwork. See yourself starting each task quickly, effortlessly moving from one job to the next.
2. **Feel the Ease:** Focus on ease and efficiency as you visualize. Picture yourself feeling motivated and focused, with each decluttering can be a journey of rediscovery, with each item representing a chapter in your life's story and feeling proud of what you've achieved.
3. **Rehearse:** Practice this visualization technique regularly, especially when you feel stuck or tempted to procrastinate. Each time you visualize success, you reinforce your confidence and reduce procrastination.

So, the next time you encounter a daunting task, take a moment to visualize yourself tackling it with ease and efficiency. This simple mental exercise can help boost your motivation and confidence, making it easier to overcome procrastination and get things done. Let's take some more examples from our daily life.

1. **Completing a Presentation:** Imagine you have an essential presentation to deliver at work. Close your eyes and visualize yourself standing

confidently before your colleagues with a clear and engaging presentation on the screen behind you. See yourself speaking with ease and clarity, capturing your audience's attention. Picture the positive reactions from your coworkers as you smoothly navigate through each slide, feeling motivated and focused. Visualize the sense of accomplishment and satisfaction as you wrap up the presentation, knowing you've delivered your message effectively and confidently.

2. **Studying for an Exam:** Imagine yourself sitting at your desk, with your surroundings all around you." textbooks and notes, preparing for a challenging exam. Visualize yourself absorbing the material effortlessly, understanding complex concepts with ease. See yourself confidently answering practice questions and solving problems, feeling motivated and focused throughout the study session. Imagine the sense of relief and accomplishment as you finish reviewing the material, knowing that you've thoroughly prepared yourself for success on the exam.

3. **Completing a Deadline-driven Project:** Envision yourself sitting at your desk, working on a deadline-driven project with multiple tasks and responsibilities. See yourself tackling each task methodically and efficiently, progressing with every step. Visualize the sense of accomplishment and satisfaction as you check off each completed job, feeling motivated and focused despite the pressure of the deadline. Picture yourself confidently meeting the project deadline with time to spare, knowing you've delivered high-quality work and exceeded expectations.

By using visualization techniques in your daily routine, whether preparing for a presentation, studying for an exam, or completing a project, you can tap into the power of your imagination to boost confidence, motivation, and productivity. Visualization helps you mentally rehearse success, making overcoming procrastination easier and achieving your goals more quickly and efficiently.

CHAPTER SIXTEEN

REWRITE YOUR INNER-DIALOGUE

Let's break down meta-modeling in a more user-friendly and engaging way:

Imagine you're facing a task you've been putting off, and negative thoughts start creeping in, like "I'll never finish this" or "I'm not good enough. Meta-modeling involves investigating and challenging negative beliefs to uncover the truth, like acting as a detective for your thoughts.

Detective Mode: When negative thoughts arise, step into your detective mode. Instead of letting them take over, ask yourself questions like, "Is this thought true?" or "What evidence do I have to support it?"

1. **Spot the Distortions:** Look for common thinking traps, like catastrophizing (imagining the worst-case scenario) or mind reading (assuming what others think). These distortions can fuel procrastination by making tasks seem scarier or more overwhelming than they are.
2. **Challenge the Thoughts:** Once you've identified a negative thought, challenge it with evidence and logic. For example, if you catch yourself catastrophizing about a project deadline, remember past successes and times when things turned out better than expected.
3. **Restructure with Empowering Thoughts:** Replace the negative thought with a more rational and empowering one. Instead of "I'll never finish this," try "I've overcome challenges before, and I have the skills to tackle this task."
4. **Practice Self-Compassion:** Remember to treat yourself with kindness. It's important to be gentle with yourself. Procrastination often stems

from fear or self-doubt, so treat yourself with the same compassion as a friend facing a similar situation.

5. **Repeat and Reinforce:** Meta-modeling, like any other skill, requires practice to master. The more you challenge and restructure your negative thoughts, the easier it becomes to shift your mindset and overcome procrastination.

Next time you catch yourself stuck in a cycle of negative thoughts and putting things off, tap into your inner detective mode instead of getting bogged down by self-criticism. Ask yourself: What made me feel this way? Are there any recurring behaviors or thoughts? By exploring these patterns, you can uncover why you're procrastinating or being hard on yourself. Once you know the root causes, you can take action to change them. It's like shining a light on a dark path—you can see where you're going and find a better way forward. With this insight, you can break free from negative cycles and move toward a more positive, productive mindset. Think of yourself as a detective on a mission to solve the mystery of your behavior, and watch as you unravel the clues to greater productivity and self-compassion. Investigate those thoughts, challenge their validity, and reframe them with a more empowering perspective. With some detective work, you'll uncover the truth behind your procrastination and pave the way for a more positive and productive mindset.

Let's relate meta-modeling to common scenarios you might encounter in daily office work:

1. **Scenario 1:** You have a big presentation coming up, and you think, "I'll never be able to deliver this effectively. I'm going to mess it up."

    - Meta-Modelling Approach: Ask yourself, "Is this thought true? Have I successfully presented before?" Challenge the negative belief by reminding yourself of past presentations where you've done well. Reframe the thought: "I have valuable insights to share and can deliver this presentation confidently."

2. **Scenario 2:** You receive constructive feedback on a project, but your initial reaction is, "I'm such a failure. I can't believe I messed this up."

   - Meta-Modelling Approach: Investigate the validity of this thought by asking, "Is it fair to label me a failure based on one setback?" Challenge the negative self-talk by acknowledging it. Remember that making mistakes is a natural part of life and that failure is not the end. Instead, it presents an opportunity for growth and learning. So, embrace your mistakes and failures, learn from them, and use them to improve yourself.

   Success is not just about avoiding failure. Mistakes are a part of learning and growth. Don't let failure discourage you. Use it as a stepping stone towards personal development. Analyze what went wrong and learn from it. Successful people learn from their mistakes and use them to make smarter choices in the future.

   It's like using a map to find a better route after getting lost. By reflecting on our mistakes or setbacks, we understand what led to the outcome and how to avoid similar pitfalls next time. These insights become valuable tools for improving our decision-making skills and navigating life's challenges more effectively. So, don't be afraid to examine your missteps—it's all part of the journey toward growth and success. So, let's embrace our mistakes and use them as opportunities for development and improvement. Mistakes are inevitable, but what sets successful people apart is their willingness to learn from them. We gather essential insights to help us make better decisions by analyzing what went wrong. So, let's embrace our mistakes and use them as opportunities for growth and improvement. With the correct thinking and attitude, failure can be a footstool for success and development. Reframe the thought: "I appreciate the feedback and will use it to improve my work in the future."

   Let us understand it better with some more examples.

3. **Scenario:** You're assigned a challenging task outside your comfort zone, and you think, "There's no way I can handle this. I'm not qualified enough."

-Meta-Modelling Approach: Investigate whether this belief is based on facts or assumptions. Challenge it by considering times when you've successfully tackled new challenges and learned. Reframe the thought, "I can't miss the chance to improve my abilities and broaden my knowledge. This opportunity is essential for my personal and professional growth.". I can approach it with curiosity and a willingness to learn."

4. **Scenario:** You're overwhelmed by your workload and think, "I'll never catch up. I'm so far behind."

-Meta-Modelling Approach: Investigate whether this belief is based on reality or exaggerated thinking. Break down the task into smaller, easily achievable steps and devise a plan to execute it accordingly. Reframe the thought: "I can prioritize my tasks and take them one step at a time. Each small achievement brings me closer to my goals."

Applying meta-modeling techniques to everyday office scenarios can help overcome procrastination and achieve goals by challenging negative beliefs and reframing thoughts.

CHAPTER SEVENTEEN

CONNECT WITH FUTURE SUCCESS

Imagine a task looming over you, like a big presentation or a daunting project deadline. Future pacing is like taking a mental trip to the future to see how awesome it feels once you've conquered that task. You're giving yourself a sneak peek into the satisfaction and pride you'll feel when it's all done.

1. Close your eyes and imagine yourself in the future after you've completed the task. Picture when you hit "send" on that crucial email or finish your presentation confidently.
2. As you visualize, tap into the emotions of satisfaction, relief, and pride. Imagine that weight lifting off your shoulders and that sense of accomplishment washing over you. Visualize yourself smiling and feeling proud of what you've achieved.
3. Now, anchor those positive feelings to the present moment. Find something tangible to remind you of that future success – a phrase, a gesture, or even a particular object on your desk.
4. Whenever you're feeling stuck or unmotivated, trigger that anchor. Remind yourself of how amazing it will feel to have completed the task. Let those future feelings of satisfaction and pride propel you into action in the present.

So, next time you're procrastinating or feeling overwhelmed by a task, take a moment to future pace. Imagine yourself on the other side, basking in the glory of a well-done job. By anchoring those positive future feelings, you'll find the motivation and drive to tackle whatever comes your way in the here and now. Here are some real-life examples to understand it better: Completing a Challenging Project:

- Scenario: You've been assigned a complex project with tight deadlines and feel overwhelmed by the workload.
- Close your eyes and envision yourself a few weeks after successfully completing the project. Picture the moment you submit the final deliverable and receive positive feedback from your team or supervisor.
- As you visualize, tap into the feelings of relief, satisfaction, and pride of accomplishing such a challenging task. Imagine the weight lifting off your shoulders and the sense of achievement washing over you.
- Choose a tangible anchor to remind you of these future feelings, such as a motivational quote on your desk or a specific song that uplifts your spirits.
- Whenever you feel demotivated or tempted to procrastinate, trigger your anchor. Remind yourself how amazing it will feel to complete the project successfully. Let those future feelings of satisfaction and pride drive you to take action in the present, whether it's diving into the next task or overcoming a hurdle.

Preparing for a Presentation:

- Scenario: You have an essential presentation and feel nervous about speaking in front of a large audience.
- Visualize yourself standing confidently before the audience, delivering your presentation with poise and clarity. "Visualize the thundering applause and the overwhelmingly positive feedback you will receive at the conclusion."
- Connect with the feelings of confidence, empowerment, and accomplishment as you envision yourself delivering a successful presentation. Picture yourself smiling and feeling proud of your performance.
- Find a tangible anchor to remind you of these future feelings, such as practicing deep breathing techniques or repeating a mantra of self-assurance before the presentation.

- When you feel pre-presentation jitters creeping in, trigger your anchor. Remember how incredible it will feel to deliver a stellar presentation and receive praise from your audience. Let those future feelings of confidence and pride motivate you to prepare diligently and approach the production with a positive mindset.

By anchoring future pacing in these examples, you can harness the power of positive visualization to overcome procrastination, boost motivation, and achieve your goals with confidence and determination.

CHAPTER EIGHTEEN

SWAP PROCRASTINATION WITH PRODUCTIVITY

Swiftly transitioning from a mental image of procrastination to one of productivity involves engaging in a deliberate mental shift akin to pressing a button or flipping a switch.

As you initiate this transition, visualize the scene of procrastination shrinking and fading away, diminishing in size and significance within your mind's eye.

Simultaneously, allow the image of productivity to expand and become more prominent, vividly depicting yourself as fully engaged in tasks, motivated, and focused. Engage your senses to make the imagery lifelike, incorporating sounds, sights, and sensations associated with both scenes. Embrace the emotional shift accompanying this transition, feeling empowered and determined to tackle your tasks with renewed vigor. With practice and repetition, mastering this technique can provide a powerful tool for overcoming procrastination and cultivating a productivity mindset.

1. **Create Mental Images:** Start by vividly imagining the scene of procrastination and productivity. For procrastination, visualize yourself engaging in behaviors like scrolling through social media or finding excuses to avoid work. For productivity, picture yourself focused, motivated, and making progress on your tasks.
2. **Notice Sensory Details:** Listen to the sensory details as you imagine each scene. What do you see, hear, feel, and smell in each scenario? Engaging your senses helps make the images more vivid and immersive.

3. **Prepare for the Swish:** Take a moment to prepare mentally. Remind yourself of your intention to overcome procrastination and embrace productivity. This mental readiness sets the stage for a smooth transition between images.

4. **Activate the Swish:** Now, as if you're pressing a mental button or flipping a switch, swiftly transition from the image of procrastination to the idea of productivity. Imagine the procrastination scene shrinking and fading away while the productive scene expands and becomes more prominent in your mind's eye.

5. **Feel the Shift:** Consider how your emotions and mindset change as you make this mental switch. Notice the sense of empowerment and motivation that comes with envisioning yourself being productive. Embrace this shift in perspective and fully embody the mindset of productivity.

6. **Reinforce the New Image:** After completing the swish, take a moment to reinforce the image of productivity in your mind. Mentally reaffirm your commitment to taking action and making progress on your tasks. Visualize yourself confidently tackling your work with focus and determination.

7. **Take Action:** With the image of productivity firmly in mind, take immediate action towards your goals. Use this newfound motivation and energy to dive into your tasks purposefully and enthusiastically. Remember that you have the power to overcome procrastination and achieve your goals.

Following these detailed steps, you can effectively use the Swish Pattern to shift from procrastination to productivity and unleash your full potential.

CHAPTER NINETEEN

ANCHORING MOTIVATIONAL STRATEGIES

Imagine your motivation as a powerful force within you, ready to propel you forward. Anchoring motivation strategies is like harnessing that force and directing it toward your goals. First, think about what lights a fire under you—is it the thrill of success, the satisfaction of making progress, or something else entirely? Once you've identified your driving force, tie it to specific tasks or activities.

For example, if achieving your goals motivates you, anchor that feeling to completing a challenging task at work. Visualize yourself crossing the finish line, feeling proud and accomplished. Then, whenever you feel tempted to procrastinate, summon that mental image. Let it reignite your motivation and push you to take action.

Motivation is the driving force behind our actions and behaviors, serving as the fuel that propels us toward our goals and aspirations. Harnessing this motivation effectively can be the key to overcoming procrastination and staying focused on the tasks. One powerful method for doing so is through anchoring motivational strategies.

Here are a few examples of different motivational strategies that you can use:

1. **Achievement:** Achievement is a common motivator, where the desire to accomplish goals and succeed is a powerful driving force. For those motivated by achievement, the satisfaction and pride of completing tasks can be a potent source of motivation. Visualizing the result, such as

checking off items on a to-do list or accomplishing milestones, can help anchor this motivation to specific tasks.

2. **Recognition:** Recognition is another powerful motivator, particularly for individuals who thrive on acknowledgment and praise from others. For them, receiving recognition for their efforts can be a significant motivator. Individuals can anchor their motivation and drive action by envisioning the appreciation and glory they may receive upon completing tasks.

3. **Personal Fulfilment:** Personal fulfillment motivates many individuals, particularly those who prioritize personal growth and development. For them, the intrinsic satisfaction and sense of pride that comes from pursuing meaningful goals can be highly motivating. By focusing on how each task contributes to their long-term happiness and fulfillment, individuals can anchor their motivation and stay committed to their objectives.

4. **Contribution:** Contribution is a motivating force for individuals who derive fulfillment from positively impacting others and the world around them. Whether through their work, volunteering, or other activities, the sense of contributing to something greater than themselves can be deeply motivating. By considering the positive impact of their tasks on their team, organization, or community, individuals can anchor their motivation and stay engaged in their work.

5. **Progress:** Progress serves as a powerful motivator for many individuals, particularly those who thrive on seeing tangible results and forward momentum. The sense of accomplishment that comes from progressing toward their goals can be highly motivating. Individuals can anchor their motivation and maintain momentum by celebrating each small victory along the way and visualizing the incremental steps they take toward their objectives.

By identifying which of these motivational strategies resonates most, you can effectively anchor your motivation to specific tasks and activities, making it easier to overcome procrastination and stay focused on achieving your goals.

Step-by-step method to anchor your motivation strategies:

1. **Identify Your Motivational Drivers:** Take some time to reflect on what truly motivates you. Is it the desire for achievement, recognition, personal fulfillment, contribution, or progress? Understanding your motivational drivers is crucial for anchoring them to specific tasks effectively.

2. **Choose Relevant Tasks:** Understand what motivates you. Is it achievement, recognition, personal fulfillment, contribution, or progress? Once you've identified your motivational drivers, select tasks or activities that align with them. For example, if you're motivated by achievement, choose tasks that allow you to set and accomplish goals. If you're seeking recognition for your abilities, it's essential to concentrate on tasks that would enable you to demonstrate your skills and gain appreciation. Showcasing your talents is the key to receiving acknowledgment. For example, if you thrive on the thrill of achievement, you might seek challenging tasks and push your limits. These could be projects that require problem-solving, creativity, or innovation. By tackling these challenges, you satisfy your craving for accomplishment and growth.

   On the other hand, if recognition is what fuels your fire, you might gravitate towards projects that allow you to showcase your skills and talents. These could be opportunities to lead a team, present your work to others, or take on high-profile assignments. Focusing on projects where your contributions are acknowledged and appreciated makes you feel valued and motivated to excel.

   In essence, picking tasks that speak to your soul means identifying activities that align with your goals and resonate with your passions and strengths. Engaging in genuinely inspiring work makes you more likely to stay motivated, focused, and fulfilled.

3. **Visualize Success:** Choose tasks that align with your motivation. If you're motivated by achievement, pick tasks where you can set and achieve goals. Visualize yourself successfully completing the chosen tasks in vivid detail. Imagine the end result, including how it feels to accomplish the mission and its positive outcomes. Use all your senses to make the visualization as realistic and compelling as possible.

4. **Associate Motivation:** Associate these tasks with your feelings of motivation. For example, link achieving a task with the joy of accomplishment. Imagine yourself successfully completing these tasks. Picture how it feels and the positive outcomes. During your

visualization, consciously connect the task with your motivational drivers. For instance, if you're visualizing completing a project, associate the feeling of achievement or recognition with that accomplishment. Anchor your motivation to the task by linking it with the positive emotions and outcomes you've visualized.

5. **Create Physical Anchors:** Use physical cues like a specific gesture or word to remind yourself of your motivation before starting a task. To reinforce the association between lessons and inspiration, create physical anchors that serve as reminders. This could be a specific gesture, word, or object you associate with your motivational drivers. Creating your personal ritual is about finding a special gesture, expression, or object that symbolizes your motivation and serves as a trigger to kickstart your inner drive. It's like having a secret weapon that you can use to harness your motivation whenever you need it most.

    For example, your personal ritual involves holding a smooth, polished stone in your hand. Whenever you're about to tackle a challenging task, you take a moment to hold the stone, feeling its solid weight and drawing strength from its presence. This simple act serves as a reminder of your inner power and determination, helping you to focus and dive into your work with renewed energy and purpose.

    Or perhaps your ritual is a specific word or phrase that holds special meaning for you. Whenever you're gearing up to tackle a task, you quietly repeat this word to yourself, letting its positive energy wash over you and propel you forward. Whether it's "focus," "perseverance," or "success," the word serves as a powerful mantra that helps you channel your motivation and overcome any obstacles in your path.

    Another example could be a physical gesture, such as clasping your hands together or standing up straight with your shoulders back. You perform this gesture whenever you're feeling unmotivated or stuck, instantly triggering a shift in your mindset and attitude. It's like flipping a switch and activating your inner powerhouse, ready to take on whatever challenges come your way.

6. **Practice Regularly:** Keep visualizing and using your reminders consistently to strengthen the connection between tasks and motivation. Consistency is vital to anchoring motivational strategies effectively—practice visualization and using physical anchors regularly to reinforce the relationship between tasks and motivation. The more you engage in these practices, the stronger the association will become.

7. **Monitor Progress:** Monitor how well these techniques work for you. Notice any changes in your motivation levels and adjust your approach accordingly. Monitoring and measuring your progress using anchoring techniques is essential to determine their effectiveness. Monitoring and measuring your progress using anchoring techniques is vital to assess their effectiveness. Notice any motivation and productivity changes as you implement these strategies. Do whatever it takes to modify your approach and attain optimal results.

8. **Celebrate Success:** Acknowledge and celebrate your progress, no matter how small. It reinforces positive behavior. Remember to celebrate your achievements, no matter how small, along the way. Please let me know if you need any further assistance. Acknowledge your progress and the effort you've put into anchoring motivational strategies. Celebrating success reinforces positive behavior and strengthens the association between tasks and motivation.

9. **Reflect and Refine:** It's important to regularly assess and adjust your methods to discover what works best for you. Evaluate your anchoring techniques to identify strengths and areas for improvement. Identify what's working well and areas for improvement. One helpful suggestion is to adjust your approach based on the feedback you receive from your observations and experiences. This way, you can ensure you're on the right track and keep progressing towards your goals.

10. **Persist and Persevere:** Anchoring motivational strategies is a process that requires time, patience, and persistence. Staying committed and continue practicing techniques, even when faced with setbacks. With dedication and perseverance, you can successfully anchor your motivational drivers to tasks and overcome procrastination effectively. Anchoring motivation takes time and practice, so keep going if you see immediate results. With persistence, you'll get there.

CHAPTER TWENTY

AFFIRMATIONS FOR PRODUCTIVITY AND SUCCESS:

1. I am in control of my time and use it wisely to achieve my goals.
2. Procrastination has no power over me; I take action with confidence.
3. I am disciplined and consistent in my efforts towards success.
4. Every task I complete brings me closer to my ultimate success.
5. I embrace challenges as opportunities for growth and learning.
6. I am focused, determined, and unstoppable in pursuing my dreams.
7. I trust myself to make the right decisions and prioritize effectively.
8. I am motivated by my vision for the future and take inspired action.
9. I overcome resistance and inertia with ease, moving forward with purpose.
10. I am resilient in the face of setbacks, always finding a way to succeed.
11. I welcome productivity and efficiency into my life every day.
12. I am fully committed to realizing my potential and living my best life.
13. I release all excuses and distractions, staying dedicated to my goals.
14. I choose progress over perfection, taking imperfect action consistently.
15. I am worthy of success, and I believe in my ability to achieve it.
16. I break tasks down into manageable steps and tackle them one by one.
17. I am proactive and proactive in seizing opportunities for growth.
18. I visualize my success and let it propel me forward with determination.
19. I surround myself with positivity and encouragement, fueling my motivation.
20. I celebrate my achievements along the way, reinforcing my progress.

21. I am accountable for my actions and take full responsibility for my results.
22. I embrace the journey of self-improvement and personal development.
23. I am unstoppable, resilient, and destined for greatness.
24. I am the architect of my destiny, creating the life I desire.
25. I am highly successful, and nothing can stand in the way of my dreams.

A Thank You Note

Thank you, dear readers, for taking the time to read this book. I sincerely hope the insights shared within these pages have added value to your life and offered you a fresh perspective on procrastination.

Remember, procrastination isn't just laziness; deeper psychological factors often influence it. By understanding the psychology behind our procrastination tendencies, we can overcome them.

I wish you a life free of procrastination and abundant and prosperous. Please use your inner strength and determination to pursue your goals passionately and purposefully. Please use your inner strength and determination to pursue your dreams with passion and purpose.

References

1. *"The Procrastination Equation: How to Stop Putting Things Off and Start Getting Stuff Done" by Piers Steel*

2. *"Eat That Frog!: 21 Great Ways to Stop Procrastinating and Get More Done in Less Time" by Brian Tracy*
3. *"Atomic Habits: An Easy & Proven Way to Build Good Habits & Break Bad Ones" by James Clear*
4. *"Deep Work: Rules for Focused Success in a Distracted World" by Cal Newport*
5. *"The Power of Habit: Why We Do What We Do in Life and Business" by Charles Duhigg*
6. *"Getting Things Done: The Art of Stress-Free Productivity" by David Allen*
7. *"Procrastinate on Purpose: 5 Permissions to Multiply Your Time" by Rory Vaden*
8. *"Indistractable: How to Control Your Attention and Choose Your Life" by Nir Eyal*
9. *"Solving the Procrastination Puzzle: A Concise Guide to Strategies for Change" by Timothy A. Pychyl*
10. *"The 5 Choices: The Path to Extraordinary Productivity" by Kory Kogon, Adam Merrill, and Leena Rinne*

9 798894 759487